Thy Face, Lord, Will I Seek

Teach Us to Pray

Anita Couser

Acknowledgments

My father, JT McCracken, my brother, Dave McCracken, my pastors, Bro. Ron Lindsey, Bro. Sam Davison, and Bro. Jason Gaddis, have been the helpers of my joy. Through their preaching, I have learned to love God and His Word. I will be eternally thankful for these men of God. I also want to thank Amanda Howerton for the artwork and my family and friends who have been a source of great help and encouragement.

Contents

Forward

Prayer is a subject that I am passionate about and has become dear to my heart. I have not arrived in my prayer life, but I am trying to cultivate it and grow it. I want God to teach me how to pray. The more time I spend with Him in prayer, I find I want more. Much of what is written on these pages is what I have gleaned from sermons and reading after others on the matter of prayer. I cannot claim to have mined out these truths on my own. There are many books on prayer, and I have not even come close to reading them all. I have put together these lessons, passing on what I have learned from others. I sure hope you can glean from them also and they will be a help to you in your prayer life. God talks to us as we read His love letter, and then we can approach His throne room, be in His presence, and talk back to Him! What an awesome gift prayer is!

1 *TEACH US TO PRAY*

Psalm 27:8 *"When thou saidst, Seek ye my face; my heart said unto thee, Thy face, LORD, will I seek."*

Matthew Henry says of this passage that David is telling of the satisfaction and benefit he experienced from seeking God's face, from communing with God in prayer. That is what this Bible study is about a prayer life that will satisfy and benefit our lives.

Seek = to search out, specifically in worship or prayer, to strive after, ask, beg, beseech, desire, enquire, get, make inquisition, procure, request, require, seek

Face = as the part that turns

LORD—Jehovah = the self-existent, eternal one

Have you ever been talking to your child and you say, "Look at me"? You want to make eye contact with them. Why? To make sure they are paying attention, to make sure they understand what you are saying. When you look into the eyes of the one you love, you want them to grasp, completely, your heart, your mind, your sincerity—all from looking face to face, eye to eye.

Do we have a prayer life that is face to face, talking to God? Just the thought of being face to face with my Maker makes me feel, um.... little. None of us deserves to have such an audience with the LORD God Almighty, yet, He desires to commune with us! He invites us into His presence, to the foot of His throne!

The Bible warns us not to pray with vain, empty repetition. We have all had those times on our cell phones when the call has dropped, but we didn't know it. Who knows how long we have been talking to....no one? That doesn't happen when we are face to face. We need to seek God's face and talk to Him with reverence and awe and know He wants to commune as a loving Father with us, His children. We need prayer that is heartfelt and sincere without pretense or show. Prayer should not be just words we mutter out of habit. We all get distracted at times when we are talking to someone, and distractions will happen while we are praying. It is important to keep seeking His face. That is why some write out their prayers as letters to God. This is why we close our eyes and bow our heads: to keep out distractions — whatever we need to do to keep our concentration and our hearts and minds on Him. We are not saying that we can't pray anytime, anywhere — sure we can. We are talking about a time set apart for the specific purpose of getting alone with God.

Psalm 105:4 *"Seek the LORD, and his strength: seek his face evermore."* **I Chronicles 16:11** *"Seek the LORD and his strength,* *seek his face continually."*

God calls us to seek His face, and we have the promise of finding His face. **Deuteronomy 4:29** *"But if from thence thou shalt seek the LORD thy God, thou shalt find him..."* **Hebrews 11:6** *"...and that he is a rewarder of them that diligently seek him."*

I have said often that I constantly need sermons, lessons, and books on prayer. I need to be challenged to have a more meaningful prayer life. We might say we need to constantly be cultivating our prayer life. We can read of great prayer warriors throughout history and say, "Wow — God heard their prayers and great things happened!" But, even after reading that, we may never surrender ourselves to that kind of discipline in our own prayer life. Ouch! That hurts, but it is the truth!

Satan does not want you and me to have a prayer life at all and he sure doesn't want us to have an effectual, fervent kind of praying that avails much. **James 5:16** *"...The effectual fervent prayer of a righteous man availeth much."* Someone has said, "Prayer is a threat to Satan's program." Satan fights against us because he knows he is defeated through prayer. A meaningful prayer life is a continual battle that is worth the fight.

"He made prayer not the preparation for the work, but the work." **Oswald Chambers.** So many people are looking for some work they can do for God, and prayer is the work we are all called to do. We are all on equal ground, have equal access to God, and are equally able to do the work, and what a wonderful, powerful work it can be.

So, do you have a meaningful, fervent prayer life? Has your heart made the choice to seek God's face? Or is it more the vain repetition, "dropped call" kind of prayer life? In one book I read, the writer said she went to a conference on prayer, and there the question was posed, *"Do you believe prayerlessness is a sin?"* If the answer is "Yes" and prayerlessness is a sin, then she had to deal with it.

II Chronicles 12:14 *"And he (*Rehoboam*) did evil, because he prepared not his heart to seek the LORD."*

Luke 18:1 *"And he spake a parable unto them to this end, that men ought always to pray, and not to faint;"*

Luke 21:36 *"Watch ye therefore, and pray always, that ye may be accounted worthy to escape all these things that shall come to pass, and to stand before the son of man."*

Luke 22:40 *"...Pray that ye enter not into temptation."*

Luke 22:46 *"...Why sleep ye? rise and pray, lest ye enter into temptation."*

I Thessalonians 5:17 *"Pray without ceasing."*

Jesus, our example, prayed often, and He commands us to pray. We could cite many more verses in the Bible that clearly teach us that we ought to pray.

So, back to the lady whose book I read. She had to agree that it was, in fact, a true statement: *prayerlessness is a sin.* The realization of this truth ended up changing her life. She had claimed that God was a priority in her life. She had to ask herself, "If that's true, why do I spend so little time with Him?" She committed to the discipline of spending an hour, every day, with the Lord.

I read her testimony and thought, *"Why don't I have this discipline in my life?"* I had made the choice to read the Bible all the way through each year and have disciplined myself to do so for many years now. Yes, it takes making the choice and having discipline — it does not happen by accident. Being faithful in attending church is the result of choice and discipline. I evaluated my prayer life, and I could say I did have a prayer life — but not one that required much discipline. I would spend hours with the Lord in prayer preparing to speak for a ladies meeting or Sunday school lesson. I would spend an hour in prayer over a heavy burden I was facing. So why not pray for an hour *every day*? This lady whose book I read was experiencing God's power and answered prayer in her life. What was I missing out on?! Have you ever looked back over your life with regret and wish you could change some things and make better decisions?

Would we still have regrets if we had started each day with meaningful prayer, asking for wisdom?

We have many examples in the Bible of people who prayed specific prayers and God heard them and answered. Hannah prayed for a child, and God heard and gave her Samuel. Elijah prayed that it would not rain; it did not rain for three years. Then, he prayed it would rain, and it did. We know that, when they sought the face of God, He turned His face to them and answered their prayers.

Sometimes we ask God for something, and we see it answered. Is that just a coincidence, or did God hear and answer our prayers? We say, "Yes, God heard and answered!" And we praise Him for it. Have any of you ever prayed about something that was not answered? Have you ever been discouraged about your prayer life or wondered if God even hears you? Is it possible to pray wrong?

Psalm 66:18 *"If I regard iniquity in my heart, the Lord will not hear me:"* **James 4:3** *"Ye ask, and receive not, because ye ask amiss, that ye may consume it upon your lusts."* **Psalm 37:4** *"Delight thyself also in the LORD; and he shall give thee the desires of thine heart."* According to these verses, there could be things that hinder our prayers, but there are also things that could help us with our prayers. Hopefully, this study will help us learn to pray or be reminded and challenged to have a more meaningful, disciplined prayer life.

Thoughts to ponder:

"All our failures are prayer failures." **John R. Rice**

"The basis of prayer is not what it costs us, but what it cost God to enable us to pray." **Oswald Chambers**

"It is not prayer that is strenuous, but the overcoming of our own laziness." **Oswald Chambers**

"He made prayer not the preparation for the work, but the work." **Oswald Chambers**

"Prayer is the key that opens and shuts heaven." **Warren Wiersbe**

"Prayer can do anything that God can do, and as God can do anything, prayer is omnipotent." **R.A. Torrey**

"Prayer is the soul's pilgrimage from self to God." **E. Hermann**

"We won't be a woman of God without being a woman of prayer." **Unknown**

"The biblical idea of prayer is that God's holiness, purpose, and wise order may be brought about." Oswald Chambers

Pray? Yes, because we are a very needy people. What is our greatest need? That God's holiness, purpose, and wise order may be brought about in our life! Prayer, meaningful prayer, the kind that takes work, discipline, and labor, is a reoccurring battle that is worth the fight.

The Lord is saying, "Look at me. Seek my face."

Luke 11:1 *"And it came to pass, that, as he was praying in a certain place, when he ceased, one of his disciples said unto him, Lord, teach us to pray..."* **Oswald Chambers** said, "They were well versed in Jewish praying, yet when they came in contact with Jesus, instead of realizing they could pray well, they came to the conclusion they did not know how to pray at all." They did not ask Jesus to teach them to preach, teach, or heal, but to pray.

Warren Wiersbe said, "The greatest argument for the priority of prayer is the fact that our Lord was a man of prayer. The disciples knew that He often prayed alone, and they wanted to learn from Him this secret of Spiritual power and wisdom. If Jesus Christ, the perfect Son of God, had to depend on prayer during "the days of his flesh" (Hebrews 5:7), then how much more do you and I need to pray! Effective prayer is the provision for every need and the solution for every problem."

"Lord, teach us to pray." Jesus gives them the model prayer. This prayer is recorded in Luke and Matthew. We are going to look at Matthew Chapter 6 and study this prayer in the chapters to follow.

Turn Your Eyes Upon Jesus

Helen H. Lemmel 1922

Turn your eyes upon Jesus,

Look full in His wonderful face,

And the things of earth will grow strangely dim,

In the light of His glory and grace.

Reflection:

Is prayerlessness a sin?

Does my current prayer life require discipline?

Do the words, *work*, *labor*, or *laziness* come to mind when I think of my prayer life?

Could God teach me anything about prayer, or do I already have the prayer life He wants for me?

Study to prepare for the next lesson:

Read Matthew 6:9-13.

In Matthew 6:9, in the phrase: *"Hallowed be thy name",* what does *hallowed* mean, according to a concordance and Webster's 1828 dictionary?

Look up "worship" in the Webster's 1828 dictionary and a concordance.

Give three examples, out of the Bible, of what worship looks like.

Listen to "God Hearing Kind of Prayer" Nov 8, 2016, Dave McCracken. This sermon is available on southwestbaptistchurch.com (Revival 2016)

Helpful resources:

e-Sword LT

Webster's 1828 Dictionary webstersdictionary1828.com
Strong's Concordance with Greek and Hebrew Lexicon

When thou saidst,
Seek ye my face;
my heart said
unto thee, Thy face,
LORD, will I seek.

PSALM 27:8

2 *TEACH US TO WORSHIP*

Matthew 6:9 *"After this manner therefore pray ye: Our Father which art in heaven, Hallowed be thy name."*

Recorded in Luke 11:1, the disciples ask Jesus to teach them to pray. Jesus then begins what has been called "The Lord's Prayer." More appropriately, this passage should be called "The Model Prayer." Jesus starts the prayer with "Our Father which art in heaven." We are not expounding on this part of the prayer, but I trust that you have been saved and are a child of God. If you have not received Jesus as your Savior, you cannot call Him "Father." You need to repent of your sin and call on Him to be your Lord and Savior — and then we get to call Him "Father"! **I John 3:1a** *"Behold, what manner of love the Father hath bestowed upon us, that we should be called the sons of God:"*

We will begin this study with the phrase "Hallowed be thy name."

> **Hallowed** = mentally venerate, think upon
>
> **Hallow** = make holy, purify, consecrate, be holy, sanctify (set apart)
>
> **Venerate** = to worship, reverence, love, see, to look upon with feeling and deep respect, revere
>
> **Worship** = to depress, that is prostrate, bow (self), down, crouch, fall down (flat), make to stoop
>
> The dictionary definition is to acknowledge the worth of another, worth-ship.

Jesus is teaching the disciples how to pray and He says, "Pray like this – start with worship." According to the definition worship is to bow physically before God; some, however, are not physically able to bow. We are to get as low as we can, with a humble attitude, heart, and mind as we acknowledge His worth. True worship will not take place without humility. If we truly see God for who He is, His worth, we will not be standing.

"Worship is the missing jewel of church today." **A. W. Tozer**
"The true nature of religious worship is seeking the face of God."
Matthew Henry

Someone said worship is not something new, but something forgotten. Jesus said it is supposed to be part of our daily prayer. Most of the time, what motivates us to pray is our request, when our proper motivation should be to worship God, the Almighty. **Oswald Chambers** said, "There is a real danger of worshipping prayer instead of praying because we worship." As we begin our prayer with worship, acknowledging who He is and all He deserves, we realize this life is all about Him. It's not about me at all. The rest of our prayer time will be put in perspective.

Have you ever seen anyone bowing before a statue? When Muslims worship, they bow toward Mecca, Saudi Arabia, five times a day. They bow toward the black stone that is there, hoping it will count in their favor on judgment day. The Buddhists worship and bow, not to an idol, but to a symbol representing the highest human potential worthy of respect. They bow as an act of humility of the heart. We know the true God, not some stone, not a symbol, but the one, true, living God. So . . . do we worship God daily? Do we bow before Him and acknowledge His worth? These other religions put most of us to shame.

I am not thanking Him for what He has done for me as though that is why I am bowing at His feet, but I'm bowing to acknowledge the truth of who He is.

There is a distinct difference between praise and worship. We will come to praising God at the end of the model prayer. We might praise a doctor for seeing us through cancer, and now we are cancer free, but we would never bow before a doctor. We know worship is for God alone. We might praise God for healing us, but worship would be acknowledging His worth even if we are never healed. Often, thanksgiving leads to worship, and worship produces thanksgiving, but the two are not the same.

This prayer goes on to say, "Give us this day our daily bread." It is truth to acknowledge prayer is to be daily. We should begin our prayer time with bowing before the Holy God and acknowledging His worth.

Matthew 6:8b-9 *". . . for your Father knoweth what things ye have need of, before ye ask him. After this manner therefore pray ye: Our Father which art in heaven, Hallowed be thy name."*

God wants us to worship Him. He already knows what we need.

John 4:23-24 *". . . for the Father seeketh such to worship him. God is a Spirit: and they that worship him must worship him in spirit and in truth."*

I do not know how to worship God *in spirit and in truth*. I ask Him to help me. My pastor, Brother Gaddis, just mentioned this verse in a message, and he said it means to worship God with integrity.

Integrity = wholeness; entireness, unbroken state, particularly of the mind, moral soundness or purity; incorruptness; uprightness; honesty.

We know perfect *truth* is God's Word. When we worship, we can recite His Word, which describes Him, back to Him, and that would be worshipping Him *in truth*. We are to humbly bow before Him with our whole, entire heart, with integrity.

We could begin with, "Dear God, I bow before you and ask you to help me worship you in spirit and in truth."

Revelation 4:11 *"Thou art worthy, O Lord, to receive glory and honour and power: for thou hast created all things, and for thy pleasure they are and were created."* **Psalm 103:1** *"Bless the LORD, O my soul: and all that is within me, bless his holy name."*

Look for scripture as you are reading His Word. Write it down, and pray it back to Him. In Brother Sam Davison's messages on worship, he said that pure worship will not take place until we are in heaven.

> Revelation 4:10-11: we will worship Him as the Creator.
> Revelation 5:7-14: we will worship Him as the Redeemer.
> Revelation 19:16: we will worship Him as the KING OF
> KINGS AND LORD OF LORDS.
> Revelation 19:4-9: we will worship Him as the Bridegroom.

We struggle with pure worship because of our sin nature and our mind that is limited and distracted so easily. Oh, but one day we will bow at His feet and worship Him without any distractions or limitations. But for now, He still wants us to worship Him daily. He is just as worthy of worship now as He will be in heaven! We can go ahead and worship Him as the Almighty Creator, as the Redeemer of all mankind, as the King of kings and Lord of lords, and as the Bridegroom!

I watched a video on the Milky Way Galaxy. The Earth is really just a tiny speck in this great galaxy that God created. And we are just a small speck on the Earth. The man who made the video said, "I am not trying to make you feel small. I am telling you, you are small." We are very small and unclean.

In Brother Sam's messages, he says that true worship will produce two results in our life: holiness and service. He used **Isaiah 6:1-8** as his text for this biblical truth.

> *"In the year that king Uzziah died I saw also the Lord sitting upon a throne, high and lifted up, and his train filled the temple. Above it stood the seraphims: each one had six wings; with twain he covered his face, and with twain he covered his feet, and with twain he did fly. And one cried unto another, and said, Holy, holy, holy , is the LORD of hosts: the whole earth is full of his glory. And the posts of the door moved at*

the voice of him that cried, and the house was filled with smoke. Then said I, Woe is me! for I am undone; because I am a man of unclean lips, and I dwell in the midst of a people of unclean lips: for mine eyes have seen the King, the LORD of hosts. Then flew one of the seraphims unto me, having a live coal in his hand, which he had taken with the tongs from off the altar: And he laid it upon my mouth, and said, Lo, this hath touched thy lips; and thine iniquity is taken away, and thy sin purged. Also I heard the voice of the Lord, saying, Whom shall I send, and who will go for us? Then said I, Here am I; send me."

Holiness — True worship will make us aware of His holiness and our unholiness. Isaiah said, "Woe is me." We will not be left unchanged if we truly worship this holy God. How I live my life matters to a holy God. He wants me to be holy. **I Peter 1:16** *"Because it is written, Be ye holy; for I am holy."*

In His holy presence, we are aware of our uncleanness; our heart is humbled, and we naturally want to get low and get clean.

Service — worship produces holy living and unreserved service. Worship and service are inseparable. Service is not an act of worship, but a result of true worship. All through the Bible worship and service go together. What I worship, I will serve. Mainly what I worship is me, myself, and I. I do not have idols I bow down to, but I sure am full of self-worth, and I am usually the one I'm busy serving. If I am too busy to serve God, I'm serving something or someone else.

Isaiah acknowledged his sinfulness, and his sin was purged. Isaiah worshipped, took care of his sin, and immediately volunteered for service. "Here am I, send me." A proper view of God provoked him to want to work for Him.

Deuteronomy 11:16 *"Take heed to yourselves, that your heart be not deceived, and ye turn aside, and serve other gods, and worship them;"* Also in Joshua 23:8 & 16 and many more verses, "worship" and "service" are mentioned together.

"If true worship is in our life, we will live a holy life, and we will serve Him. Now make your request. God grants the request of those who worship Him. True worship and humility before God will dictate the nature of your request." **Sam Davison**

"The biblical idea of prayer is that God's holiness, purpose, and wise order may be brought about." **Oswald Chambers**

Will you commit to worship God this week for five minutes a day? You might ask, "Why five minutes?" The longer we bow before Him, the more we are dwelling on the truth of who He is. I can be done in about thirty seconds, but committing to worship longer causes me to dig deeper and cultivate a more meaningful worship time.

"Lord God Omnipotent, how my soul delights to know that you care for sparrows and number the hairs of our head! Lord, breathe on me till I am in the frame of mind and body to worship you. O Lord, I would seek your face now, but what good is my seeking if you do not reveal yourself? Show me your face, O Lord. Keep me ever seeing you." **Oswald Chambers**

"Consider brethren, we have been called to come boldly into this place — this room where God sits upon His throne, surrounded by the four beasts and the twenty-four elders, and where the cherubim repeat, "Holy, holy, holy, Lord God Almighty, which was, and is, and is to come" (Revelation 4:8) while the seraphim weave their own glorious melody around the holy refrain, how can we come boldly into this room?" **Jerry Scheidbach**

Psalm 95:6 *"O come, let us worship and bow down: let us kneel before the LORD our maker."*

Matthew 6:9

"..Our Father which art in heaven, Hallowed be thy name."

Elohim — The Mighty and Powerful Creator, who is of power to create and keep covenants. It is a plural noun, meaning God is plural (Father, Son, Holy Ghost), yet one in unity. Translated as "God." Genesis 1:1-5.

Jehovah — The Self-sufficient, Self-existent One, who reveals Himself to His creation. Translated as "GOD" or "LORD." Isaiah 12:1-6.

El-Shaddai — The All-Sufficient Mighty One, who is the strength-giver and satisfier of His people so that they might be fruitful for His glory. Genesis 17:1-8; Exodus 6:2-3.

Adonai — Owner, Master, and Lord, with unrestricted authority and control over His creation. Translated as "Lord." Psalm 110:1.

Jehovah-Jireh — The LORD who sees and foresees, and who provides for the need He sees. Genesis 22:1-14.

Jehovah-Rophe — The GOD who heals, morally and spiritually as well as physically; the One who gives cure and comfort. Pronounced "*raw'-faw*" Exodus 15:20-26.

Jehovah-Nissi — The LORD is our banner of victory. Pronounced "*niss'-i*" Exodus 17:8-16.

Jehovah-M'Kaddesh — The LORD who sanctifies; sets us apart from the bondage of sin and the condemnation of the world. Leviticus 20:1-8.

Jehovah-Tsidkenu – The Righteous GOD, who is our righteousness. Pronounced "*sid-kay'-noo*" Jeremiah 23:1-6.

Jehovah-Rohi — The LORD who tends, leads, feeds, and shepherds. Pronounced "*row'-hee*" Psalm 23:1-6.

Jehovah-Shalom — The LORD is peace. He is our peace and the One who provides our safety, wellness, happiness, health, and prosperity. Judges 6:1-6, 22-24.

Jehovah-Shammah — The LORD who is present; He is there for His own. Ezekiel 48:30-35.

El-Elyon — The God who is the strongest of the strong, the mightiest of the mighty, the greatest of the great; the Most High God. Genesis 14:17-24.

Jehovah-Sabaoth — The Lord of hosts, who has all the angelic armies He needs to fight for us and defeat our foes. Psalm 89:1-8

Qadowsh-Iysh –The Holy One; the GOD who is separate, set apart, other than and who knows no equal or rival. Pronounced "*kaw-dōsh'eesh*" Isaiah 12:1-6.

Qanna – The Jealous GOD, who is provoked to jealousy when His people give their devotion to that which is not God. Pronounced "*kaw-naw*" Exodus 20:1-6, 34:10-17.

Almighty, Unchangeable God

Cindy Berry 1949

Who spread out the clouds before Him?
Who fashioned the earth with His hands?
Who created the starry host,
And formed the earth at His command?
Who scatters lightning before Him,
Commands the rain and snow to fall?
Who makes the nations tremble?
Who is Lord over all?

He is Almighty, Unchangeable God,
King of kings, Lord of lords, robed in majesty.
He rules and reigns, for all eternity,
Almighty, Unchangeable God.

He is like the light at sunrise,
Like the brightness after the rain.
Robed in splendor,
He's seated on His heavenly throne above.
His glory fills the heavens;
He is exalted over all.
Yet this God of Heaven loves me
With an everlasting love.

Reflection:

Why should I worship God?

Will I commit to worship God five minutes a day this week?

How many of you make a prayer list? According to Jesus, the first thing on our list should be to worship our Father.

Study to prepare for the next lesson:

Matthew 6:10 *"Thy kingdom come. Thy will be done in earth as it is in heaven."*

According to a concordance, what is the definition for "will"?

What is the definition for "surrender" according to Webster's 1828 dictionary?

Write out these verses: Luke 9:24; Romans 12:1; I Corinthians 6:20; II Corinthians 5:15.

Give three examples, out of the Bible, of people who surrendered to the will of God. Several of these are listed in Hebrews Chapter 11.

When thou saidst,
Seek ye my face;
my heart said
unto thee, Thy face,
LORD, will I seek.

PSALM 27:8

3 *TEACH US TO SURRENDER*

Matthew 6: 10 *"Thy kingdom come. Thy will be done in earth, as it is in heaven."*

Can we pray? "God, I want your perfect will in my life, whatever that may look like. I surrender."

Will = desire, pleasure

Surrender = To yield to the power of another; to give or deliver up possession upon compulsion or demand; to yield; to give up; to resign in favor of another; as, to surrender a right or privilege.

We look at the examples of the Old Testament saints who surrendered, and we see how things turn out for them. It was wonderful — God came through for each of them. Were they scared, sad, or possibly nervous about the unknown? Yes, I'm sure they were. Abraham, Hannah, Esther, Ruth, Daniel, the Hebrew boys, Joseph, and many more have stories that end with praise to the Lord for His faithfulness, deliverance, and blessing.

These are definitely testimonies of what surrender looks like. They surrendered their will, life, and comfort to God's will.

We can look to Jesus *for an example of total surrender.* **Philippians 2:8** *"And being found in fashion as a man, he humbled himself, and became obedient unto death, even the death of the cross."* **Hebrews 12:2** *"Looking unto Jesus the author and finisher of our faith; who for the joy that was set before him endured the cross, despising the shame, and is set down at the right hand of the throne of God."* The result of Jesus' surrender to the cross, surrender to the will of the Father, was the joy of the Lord, the salvation of souls, and peace between God and man!

Although we do see God work many miracles through the surrendered lives of the New Testament apostles, unlike the Old Testament saints, they had a different ending. It is recorded in history that eleven of the twelve apostles died some sort of martyr's death.

I do not believe all who enter God's heaven will hear, **Matthew 25:21** *"His lord said unto him, Well done, thou good and faithful servant...enter thou into the joy of thy lord"*, but I do believe those that have died for the cause of Christ have heard these words.

These men lived out the discipleship mentioned in **Luke 14:33b** *"...whosoever he be of you that forsaketh not all that he hath, he cannot be my disciple."*

> **Disciple** = a learner, pupil, a follower
>
> **Forsaketh** = to bid farewell, forsake, take leave, send away (surrender)

"Our motivation for surrender should not be for any personal gain. Genuine to surrender is a personal, sovereign, preference for Jesus Christ." **Oswald Chambers**

The first part of Matthew 6:10 starts with, *"Thy kingdom come."* This is to say, even so, come Lord Jesus! We are to live as though Jesus were coming today! If we knew God was taking us to heaven today, I don't believe any of us would struggle with surrender. We would surrender all and be willing to pay any price for Him. That is exactly where God wants us to live daily. It puts everything into perspective when we consider the rapture could happen today. We are just pilgrims passing through. This world is not our home, heaven is. Someone said, "We should live like Jesus died yesterday, rose from the dead today, and is returning tomorrow."

We sing "I Surrender All" and "Wherever He Leads I'll Go." These hymns might be easy for us to sing, but to live them . . . not so easy.

> **Luke 14:25-33** *"And there went great multitudes with him: and he turned, and said unto them, If any man come to me, and hate not his father, and mother, and wife, and children, and brethren, and sisters, yea, and his own life also, he cannot be my disciple. And whosoever doth not bear his cross, and come after me, cannot be my disciple. For which of you, intending to build a tower, sitteth not down first, and counteth the cost, whether he have sufficient to finish it? Lest haply, after he hath laid the foundation, and is not able to*

finish it, all that behold it begin to mock him, Saying, This man began to build, and was not able to finish…..So likewise, whosoever he be of you that forsaketh not all that he hath, he cannot be my disciple."

To be a disciple means God is your Lord and Master. Jesus is preaching to a crowd that was not the least bit interested in spiritual things. He preaches personal discipleship. This discipleship is for believers who are willing to pay the price. Consider the cost to love Christ above all else.

Bro. Sam Davison says of this passage, "There are no shortcuts to true discipleship. The cross is a place of sacrifice and dying to self. Jesus sets the standard for discipleship."

Jesus says to follow Him with a perfect heart. Having a perfect heart means with a whole heart, withholding nothing from God. It is total surrender. Carry the cross? It means death to self, death to our own plans and ambitions, and willingness to serve Him as He leads.

Jesus was on His way to Jerusalem when He spoke these words in Luke 14. Look what happened to Him there. He does not ask us to do anything for Him that He has not already done for us. Jesus is the ultimate example of surrender, and He considered the cost. **Matthew 26:42** *"He went away again the second time, and prayed, saying, O my Father, if this cup may not pass away from me, except I drink it, thy will be done."*

II Corinthians 5:15 *"And that he died for all, that they which live should not henceforth live unto themselves, but unto him which died for them, and rose again."*

I Corinthians 6:20 *"For ye are bought with a price: therefore glorify God in your body, and in your spirit, which are God's."*

God is not Lord, we have not surrendered, when we are fighting for our rights.

I have no rights. God owes me nothing. I deserve nothing.

I am not my own. Everything that I would call mine is God's. I cannot claim ownership of anything or anyone. Our prayer and attitude should be, "I surrender everything in my life to you, God, for you to do whatever you need, to make me a disciple and make me useful for your service. I surrender all that thy will may be done. Thy will be done in earth as it is in heaven."

Romans 12: 1-2 *"I beseech thee therefore, brethren, by the mercies of God, that ye present your bodies a living sacrifice, holy, acceptable unto God, which is your reasonable service. And be not conformed to this world: but be ye transformed by the renewing of your mind, that ye may prove what is that good, and acceptable, and perfect, will of God."*

Remember the rich young ruler in **Luke 18:22-23**, *"...Yet lackest thou one thing: sell all that thou hast, and distribute unto the poor, and thou shalt have treasure in heaven: and come, follow me. And when he heard this, he was very sorrowful: for he was very rich."* This man considered the cost and then walked away from the One who could give him eternal riches.

Luke 9:24 *"For whosoever will save his life shall lose it: but whosoever will lose his life for my sake, the same shall save it."*

"He is no fool who gives what he cannot keep to gain what he cannot lose." **Jim Elliot**

He is a fool who keeps fighting and struggling for that which he cannot keep. Surrender spares us from worry. I do not own anything, it is all God's. Ownership causes worry. Surrender brings peace and joy. What God owns He takes care of. Surrender is a choice. God does not make us surrender to Him. If we are worried, we are not surrendered. If we are grumbling and complaining, we are not surrendered. If we do not have peace, we are not surrendered.

Many of you might be familiar with "The Pineapple Story." It is a true story. I will give a brief synopsis of the account.

It is about Otto Koning, a missionary ministering to people who live in a jungle. He is frustrated because they steal from him — they steal everything. It is hard for him to grow anything because of the climate but, finally, he gets pineapple to grow. It takes three years from the time he plants them until they produce fruit. Finally, there is fruit, but he does not get even one because the people take them all. He tries to tell them that they are stealing and that it is not right for them to steal, so they call him "the angry missionary." He *is* angry. He is fed up and ready to quit. Otto goes home on furlough and does not intend to go back. While on furlough, he hears a message about surrender, gets convicted, and gives the pineapples to God. He then goes back to the people, and this time he has joy — he is no longer angry. The people see the difference in him and say, "You must be a Christian." The people keep stealing, but he tells them that they are God's pineapples. The people were not finding pigs to hunt, they were not catching fish, and their babies were getting sick. They realize it was because they were stealing from God. First, they asked Otto to take the pineapples back from God, so they could steal from Otto again. Then, they quit stealing and started returning things to Otto. God got the glory.

You need to read the story! (You can see Otto tell the story on youtube.com, or the story is available to read online.) At the end of the story, Otto asks, "What is in your pineapple garden?" We have nothing to surrender to the Lord that isn't already His. Why don't we put our palms up to God and surrender: my life, my family, my possessions, my dreams, my hopes, my plans, my frustrations, my disappointments, my heartache, my time, my talents, my treasures, ... everything that I would call mine?

"Lord, I surrender all to follow you. Show me things in my life that I have not surrendered to you. Lord, I want your perfect will in my life that I might be the disciple you want me to be; that I might be used for your honor and glory. Not my will, but Thy will be done."

"We would want for our lives, what God wants for our lives if we were wise enough to want it." (Unknown) Why does it scare us so badly when we know how much He loves us?!

Selfishness *vs.* surrender — the opposite of surrender is selfishness. If we do not make a purposeful effort to surrender, our nature of selfishness will prevail. If we say, "It will *cost* me? No thanks." We will miss out on God's will and purpose for our life.

"The biblical idea of prayer is that God's holiness, purpose, and wise order may be brought about." **Oswald Chambers**

Hebrews 12:2 *"Looking unto Jesus the author and finisher of our faith; who for the joy that was set before him endured the cross, despising the shame, and is set down at the right hand of the throne of God."*

"Is Your All on the Altar?" What do you need to place on the altar of surrender? What is in your pineapple garden?

Is Your All on the Altar?

Elisha A. Hoffman –1900

You have longed for sweet peace,
And for faith to increase,
And have earnestly, fervently prayed;
But you cannot have rest,
Or be perfectly blest,
Until all on the altar is laid.

Refrain:
Is your all on the altar of sacrifice laid?
Your heart does the Spirit control?
You can only be blest,
And have peace and sweet rest,
As you yield Him your body and soul.

Would you walk with the Lord,
In the light of His word,
And have peace and contentment alway?
You must do His sweet will,
To be free from all ill,
On the altar your all you must lay.

Oh, we never can know
What the Lord will bestow
Of the blessings for which we have prayed,
Till our body and soul
He doth fully control,
And our all on the altar is laid.

Who can tell all the love
He will send from above,
And how happy our hearts will be made;
Of the fellowship sweet
We shall share at His feet,
When our all on the altar is laid.

Reflection:

Listen to or read *The Pineapple Story*.

Make a list of everything and everyone that God wants you to surrender to Him.

Words to a song by Brian Free, **"I just want to please You, Lord; be in Your will in every way; to be lost in Your presence, found in Your likeness and hear You say well done some day."** Is this your prayer?

Will you make a commitment to pray every day, surrendering all on you "my" list? Will you acknowledge that you have no rights, that He owes you nothing and that you deserve nothing?

Study to prepare for the next lesson:

Matthew 6:11 *"Give us this day our daily bread."*

What do you need *today*, not tomorrow, *today*?

According to Ephesians 6:10-18, why do we need to put on the armour of God?

List the six pieces of the armour of God.

Would praying on this armour be a *daily* need?

Write out these verses: John 17:17; Ephesians 4:24; Mark 16:15; I John 5:4; James 1:8; Ephesians 5:18. (Each verse has a truth about the armour of God.)

When thou saidst,
Seek ye my face;
my heart said
unto thee, Thy face,
LORD, will I seek.

PSALM 27:8

4 *TEACH US TO DEPEND ON YOU*

Matthew 6:11 *"Give us this day our daily bread."*

The word "bread" in verse 11 means bread, or food. God is aware that we have physical needs and promises to supply all of them. **Philippians 4:19** *"But my God shall supply all your need..."*

"Daily bread" is a term that indicates that God wants us to acknowledge our dependence on Him daily. God fed the children of Israel manna each day and warned them not to try to store up manna for the future. He would supply their need daily.

 "Ask for daily bread, which teaches us not to take thought for tomorrow." **Matthew Henry**.

Matthew 6:34a *"Take therefore no thought for the morrow: for the morrow shall take thought for the things of itself."*

We need to come to Him daily. God knows what we need. He asks

33

us to worship Him, surrender our all to Him, and ask what we will from Him. He wants to meet our needs today.

God invites us to come and make our request. **John 16:24** *"Hitherto have ye asked nothing in my name: ask, and ye shall receive, that your joy may be full."*

His mother asked Him to make wine. Many asked for physical healing. Paul asked for his infirmity to be taken away — more than once. God invites us to ask for our heart's desires. So ask!

We are warned against asking to consume upon our own lust. **James 4:3** *"Ye ask, and receive not, because ye ask amiss, that ye may consume it upon your lusts."* We should ask according to His will. **I John 5:14** *"And this is the confidence that we have in him, that, if we ask any thing according to his will, he heareth us:"* **Romans 8:26-27** *"Likewise the Spirit also helpeth our infirmities: for we know not what we should pray for as we ought: but the Spirit itself maketh intercession for us with groanings which cannot be uttered. And he that searcheth the hearts knoweth what is the mind of the Spirit, because he maketh intercession for the saints according to the will of God."*

Hebrews 4:16 *"Let us therefore come boldly unto the throne of grace, that we may obtain mercy, and find grace to help in the time of need."*

**God is aware of our physical needs,
but our spiritual needs are His main concern.**

We need to depend on Him *daily* for our spiritual needs as well. We cannot store up on Sunday all that we need for the rest of the week. So, what is our greatest need today? There is a passage of

scripture that tells us exactly what to ask for daily.
Ephesians 6:10-18.

"The armour of God, provided by God, is the source of everything
we *need.*" **Sam Davison**

We are going to work our way through Ephesians 6:10-18 and see
how praying on the armour of God meets every spiritual need. It
does not say we have to put this on every day, but can you tell me
which day would be safe not to put this armour on?

Ephesians 6:14a *"Stand therefore, having your loins girt about
with truth..."*

> The Belt of Truth. This is the first part of the armour listed, and
> it is the piece that supports the weapons. A girdle
> restrains, and truth restrains. The Word of God is truth.
> When Jesus was tempted in the wilderness by Satan, He
> used the Word. He was tempted with the lust of the eye,
> the lust of the flesh, and the pride of life. The truth
> restrained Jesus from falling into temptation. Matthew
> Henry says the truth restrains us from indulgence in lust
> and excessive indulgence of liberty. Truth restrains us from
> falling for Satan's lies, his temptations. The only way we
> know what a lie is, is to know what truth is. We need to
> know God's Word and put It on. The victory over Satan is
> going to be in proportion to how much of the Word we
> know. Every sermon we hear, every time we read God's
> Word, every song that speaks truth, every Bible lesson,
> every book based on the truth is how we gain restraint
> against Satan's lies. We need to know truth so we can
> combat the lies of Satan. We need to read it and memorize
> it. We really can't afford to miss one church service, one

Sunday school lesson, or one day of reading the Bible.

John 17:17 *"Sanctify them through thy truth: thy word is truth."*

John 8:32 & 44 *"And ye shall know the truth, and the truth shall make you free." "Ye are of your father the devil...because there is no truth in him...for he is a liar, and the father of it."*

Psalm 119:128 *"Therefore I esteem all thy precepts concerning all things to be right; and I hate every false way."*

"Dear God, give me the belt of truth. Your Word is truth. Help me to know your Word and apply the truth of your Word today. Help me to have discernment to know the difference between a lie and truth. Help me to be a woman of truth, to speak your truth, and know your truth."

Do I need to know truth today? Yes!

Ephesians 6:14b *"... and having on the breastplate of righteousness;"*

The Breastplate of Righteousness. We need our heart protected. If Satan gets our heart, he has our life. **Ephesians 4:24** *"And that ye put on the new man, which after God is created in righteousness and true holiness."* **Proverbs 15:28-29** *"The heart of the righteous studieth to answer: but the mouth of the wicked poureth out evil things. The LORD is far from the wicked: but he heareth the prayer of the righteous."* **Matthew 5:6** *"Blessed are they which do hunger and thirst after righteousness: for they shall be filled."* **Matthew 6:33** *"But seek ye first the kingdom of God, and his righteousness; and all these things shall be added unto you."*

"Dear God, help me to put on your righteousness today. I have no righteousness of my own, but I have your righteousness. Help me to be right with you and right with others today. Help me to do right and be right according to what your standard of right is. Help me to seek and hunger and thirst after righteousness."

Do we need His righteousness today? Yes!

Ephesians 6:15 *"And your feet shod with the preparation of the gospel of peace;"*

> Shoes of the gospel of peace. Be prepared to share the gospel, the good news of peace, on purpose, and look for opportunities. **Mark 16:15b** *"...Go ye into all the world, and preach the gospel to every creature."* **Jude 1:22** "And of some have compassion, making a difference:"

"Dear God, help me be prepared to share your gospel today. Give me boldness when you prompt me. Help me to see the needs of everyone I come in contact with today. Help me to have compassion and make a difference in the lives of others today."

Do people around us have needs? Do I need God's help, to be a help to others today? Yes!

Ephesians 6:16 *"Above all, taking the shield of faith, wherewith ye shall be able to quench all the fiery darts of the wicked."*

> The Shield of Faith. **Hebrews 11:33 & 34** *"Who through faith subdued kingdoms, wrought righteousness, obtained promises, stopped the mouths of lions, Quenched the violence of fire, escaped the edge of the sword, out of weakness were made strong, waxed valiant in fight, turned to flight the armies of the aliens."* **Hebrews 11:6a** *"But without faith it is impossible to please him:"* **I John 5:4b** *"...this is the victory that over cometh the world, even our*

faith." **Hebrews 12:2a** *"Looking unto Jesus the author and finisher of our faith;"* More necessary than all is faith in God. This piece of the armour can move to wherever we need the protection. Faith is the victory that extinguishes all of Satan's arsenal! Satan throws darts of doubt — the opposite of doubt is faith.

"Dear God, give me faith today. Help me to trust you completely. Give me the kind of faith that pleases you and protects me from Satan."

Do I need faith today? Yes, above all!

Ephesians 6:17a *"And take the helmet of salvation…"*

The Helmet of Salvation. Salvation here means "defender," "defense." We need our minds protected. **James 1:8** *"A double minded man is unstable in all his ways."* **Philippians 4:8** *"Finally, brethren, whatsoever things are true, whatsoever things are honest, whatsoever things are just, whatsoever things are pure, whatsoever things are lovely, whatsoever things are of good report; if there be any virtue, and if there be any praise, think on these things."* Right thinking protects me from wrong living.

"Dear God, help me to think the way you would have me to think today. Give me your mind about circumstances and people. Help me to make good decisions today. Give me wisdom and understanding that comes from you."

How is that for meeting some need we will have today? Do I need the mind of God today? Yes!

Ephesians 6:17b *"…and the sword of the Spirit, which is the word of God:"*

The Sword of the Spirit. We need this weapon to fight Satan. The Word of God. If we are filled with the Spirit, God is in control, and Satan does not have a chance. We are commanded to be full of the Spirit. **Ephesians 5:18b** *"...be filled with the Spirit;"* The account in Luke, when Satan was tempting Jesus, says, *"And Jesus being full of the Holy Ghost returned from Jordan, and was led by the Spirit into the wilderness, Being forty days tempted of the devil..."* **Luke 4:1-2a**, Jesus used the Word of God to defeat Satan. This is the same Spirit we are to be filled with. The Spirit helps us obey the Word of God and defeat Satan's temptations. We cannot fight him in our own strength.

"Dear God, fill me with your Holy Spirit today. Empty me of me and my wicked flesh. Fill me from the top of my head to the bottom of my feet, and keep filling me throughout the day. Control my mouth and my actions that you might bring honor and glory to yourself through me today."

Do I need God's Spirit to control me today? Yes!

What more could I need today? We can have victory over Satan and have a life that is useful for God — a victorious, Spirit-filled, and Spirit-led life, of truth, wisdom, faith, righteousness, and peace! The Word of God is called "the bread of life."

The Word is entwined with each piece of this armour. Each piece is truth from God's Word that protects and satisfies our souls. We can be filled with the bread of life daily. Tomorrow we will have needs, and we will be hungry again. We need to acknowledge our dependence on Him daily. "Give us this day our daily bread."

I Need Thee Every Hour

Annie Hawks and Robert Lowry 1872

I need Thee every hour, most gracious Lord;
No tender voice like Thine can peace afford.

Refrain:
I need Thee, oh, I need Thee;
Every Hour I need Thee;
Oh, bless me now, my Savior,
I come to Thee.

I need Thee every hour, stay Thou nearby;
Temptations lose their pow'r when Thou art nigh.

I need Thee every hour, in joy or pain;
Come quickly and abide, or life is vain.

I need Thee every hour; teach me Thy will;
And Thy rich promises in me fulfill.

I need Thee every hour, most Holy One;
Oh, make me Thine indeed, Thou blessed Son.

Reflection:

"The armour of God, provided by God, is the source of everything we need." **Sam Davison**

Will you commit to pray on the armour of God every day?

Study to prepare for the next lesson:

Matthew 6:12 *"And forgive us our debts, as we forgive our debtors."*

Write out these verses: Matthew 6:14-15; Matthew 18:35; Mark 11:25-26; Luke 17:3-4.

Write out the *Ten Commandments* from Exodus 20.

In Psalm 66:18, what does the word "regard" mean, according to a concordance?

Read I John 1:8-10.

When thou saidst,
Seek ye my face;
my heart said
unto thee, Thy face,
LORD, will I seek.

PSALM 27:8

5 *TEACH US TO REPENT*

Matthew 6:12 *"And forgive us our debts, as we forgive our debtors."*

The word "and" is the understanding that "Today I have needs, and today I need forgiveness."

In this part of the prayer, we are asking God to forgive us only as we are willing to forgive others. This is a good reminder for us not to let "un-forgiveness" creep in. The Bible is clear in that we are to forgive others — always.

Matthew 6:14-15 *"For if ye forgive men their trespasses, your heavenly Father will also forgive you: But if ye forgive not men their trespasses, neither will your Father forgive your trespasses."*

Matthew 18:34-35 *"And his lord was wroth, and delivered him to the tormentors, till he should pay all that was due unto him. So* *likewise shall my heavenly Father do also unto you, if ye from your hearts forgive not everyone his brother their trespasses."*

Mark 11:25-26 *"And when ye stand praying, forgive, if ye have ought against any: that your Father also which is in heaven may forgive you your trespasses. But if ye do not forgive, neither will your Father which is in heaven forgive your trespasses."*

Luke 17:3-4 *"Take heed to yourselves: If thy brother trespass against thee, rebuke him; and if he repent, forgive him. And if he trespass against thee seven times in a day, and seven times in a day turn again to thee, saying, I repent; thou shalt forgive him."*

Colossians 3:13 *"Forbearing one another, and forgiving one another, if any man have a quarrel against any: even as Christ forgave you, so also do ye."*

Ephesians 4:32 *"And be ye kind one to another, tenderhearted, forgiving one another, even as God for Christ's sake hath forgiven you."*

Forgive = cry, forsake, lay aside, leave, let, omit, put away, suffer, yield up.

God is serious about forgiveness. If I am not in fellowship with God, I cannot pray effectively. These scriptures leave zero room for exceptions — none! Again, this might be easy to say or write, but in real life, it could be very hard. God can help us forgive. He has said we can do *all* things through Christ. Philippians 4:13

"The world's worst prison is the prison of an unforgiving heart."
Warren Wiersbe

We know that un-forgiveness brings bitterness and that our fellowship with God will be broken. That is the most miserable and dangerous place a Christian can be.

> "He was not teaching that believers earned God's forgiveness by forgiving others, for this would be contrary to God's free grace and mercy. When we forgive each other, we are not earning the right to prayer. Forgiveness belongs to the matter of fellowship: if I am not in fellowship with God, I cannot pray effectively. Since prayer involves glorifying God's name, hastening the coming of God's kingdom and helping to accomplish God's will on earth, the one praying must not have sin in his heart. If God answered the prayers of a believer who had an unforgiving spirit, He would dishonor His own name. How could God work through such a person to get His will done on earth? If God gave him his request, He would be encouraging Sin!" **Warren Wiersbe**

"When our hearts are humble and repentant, we will gladly forgive our brothers. But where there is pride and desire for revenge, there cannot be true repentance, and this means God cannot forgive. We must experience God's forgiveness in our hearts so that it humbles us and makes us gentle and forgiving toward others." **Warren Wiersbe**

"What an unforgiving person actually prays is this: "Deal with me as I have dealt with others." **Haddon Robinson**

"Those who come to God for the forgiveness of their sins against Him must make conscience of forgiving those who have offended them, else they curse themselves when they say the Lord's Prayer." **Matthew Henry**

"We are never more like God than when, for Christ's sake, we extend forgiveness fully and freely to those who have sinned against us." **Haddon Robinson**

We must forsake, lay aside, leave, omit, put away, yield up — FORGIVE — all trespasses against us.

"Dear God, help me be a forgiving person. Show me if I have an unforgiving spirit."

Now, we are ready to ask for forgiveness. "Forgive us our debts."

Psalm 66:18 *"If I regard iniquity in my heart, the Lord will not hear me:"*

Regard = to see, consider, enjoy, gaze, take heed

Iniquity = trouble, vanity, wickedness, evil, false, idol, mischief, unjust, unrighteous

---

"The verb "regard" means to recognize and cherish, to be unwilling to confess and forsake known sin. It means approving that which God condemns. When we recognize sin in our hearts, we must immediately judge it, confess it, and forsake it; otherwise, the Lord can't work on our behalf. To cover sin is to invite trouble and discipline." **Warren Wiersbe**

Hebrews 12:6 *"For whom the Lord loveth he chasteneth, and scourgeth every son whom he receiveth."*

"We should declare unto those that fear God, what He has done for our souls, and how He has heard and answered our prayers, inviting them to join us in prayer and praise; this will turn to our mutual comfort, and to the glory of God. We cannot share these spiritual privileges, if we retain the love of sin in our hearts, though we refrain from the gross practice, sin, regarded in the heart, will spoil the comfort and success of prayer; for the sacrifice of the wicked is an abomination of the Lord. But if the feeling of sin in the heart causes desires to be rid of it; if it be the presence of one urging a demand we know we must not, cannot comply with, this is an argument of sincerity. And when we pray in simplicity and godly sincerity, our prayers will be answered. This will excite gratitude to Him who hath not turned away our prayer nor His mercy from us. It was not prayer that fetched the deliverance, but His mercy that sent it. That is the foundation of our hopes, the fountain of our comforts, and ought to be the matter of our praises." **Matthew Henry**

God will not turn His face to us and bless us if we have known sin in our life that we are justifying and not confessing as sin, or if we are living a life indulging in things we know are contrary to the Word of God. For example, if we hear a message on tithing, right out of God's Word, but we say, "No, I cannot, and I will not give ten percent of my income to God." The same would be true of fornication, cussing, drinking, gossip, lying, overspending, laziness, etc. We are not saying, "I have forsaken every sin." We are saying, "I acknowledge this is sin in my life, God. I agree with you that it is sin, and I repent of it and ask you to change me and help me forsake this sin in my life."

I John 1:8-10 *"If we say that we have no sin, we deceive ourselves, and the truth is not in us. If we confess our sins, he is faithful and just to forgive us our sins, and to cleanse us from all unrighteousness. If we say that we have not sinned, we make him a liar, and his word is not in us."*

Jeremiah 17:9 *"The heart is deceitful above all things, and desperately wicked: who can know it?"*

We are not okay! We all have sin to confess — daily.

It is more than saying, "Forgive us our sin and our shortcomings today, Lord." We are praying face to face with our Lord and Savior. It is hard to look into the eye of someone you have sinned against until you make it right. We need to come to the Savior and confess our sin. Name the sin. You do not want someone to say to you they are sorry and not be specific. We teach our children to say they are sorry for "hitting" the other person, or for whatever the offense was. That is how we are to come to God. We are to name our sin and confess it to His face.

We talked about coming into the presence of a Holy God in worship and seeing our sinful selves, like Isaiah, "woe is me." The closer we get to God, the more our sin looks like the gross sin that it is. I will say it again: WE ARE NOT OKAY!

What does "confess" mean? It means much more than simply to "admit" sin. We are to say the same thing about our sin that God says about it. To confess is to acknowledge and call sin what God calls sin: envy, hatred, lust, deceit, pride, stealing, etc.

We wrote out the Ten Commandments in our Bible study, and this is a good place to start in order to see our sinful state and confess sin. We are going to briefly touch on each one of the Commandments and agree with God on what sin is. Much of these are excerpts from Bro. Sam Davison's lessons on the Ten Commandments.

1st Commandment — Exodus 20:3 *"Thou shalt have no other gods before me."*

To love anything more than God is to make it a god. We talked about surrender; if we are not willing to surrender fully to God, then something is a god in our life.

Do you have your own kingdoms that you are controlling? Are you on the throne of your life? Let's go ahead and call it SIN.

"I fear upon search, we have more idolaters among us than we are aware of." **Thomas Watson**

"Dear God, forgive me for having other gods before you. I know I let things and others come before you (name them). Mainly, I am the god I put before you. Forgive me."

2nd Commandment — Exodus 20:4-6 *"Thou shalt not make unto thee any graven image."*

Qanna — God is a jealous God. We might not have a crucifix or a statue, but a more "sophisticated" violation in principle is the same. The devotion and affection given to a career, sport, hobby, money, entertainment, or anything else becomes the graven image. We do not have time to devote to God, but we have time for everything else, Facebook, TV, the gym, etc. Let's acknowledge this in our life and call it SIN.

Romans 1:25 *"Who changed the truth of God into a lie, and worshipped and served the creature more than the Creator …"*

"God forbids us to give our hearts to the service of any but Him." **Carroll Simcox**

"Dear God, forgive me for worshipping the creature more than you, the Creator. You are a jealous God, and I have been devoted to things instead of you."

3rd Commandment — Exodus 20:7 *"Thou shalt not take the name of the LORD thy God in vain;"*

No doubt many of us are guilty of the light-hearted use of the name of God. We must let the Word of God govern our use of God's holy name. We are not guiltless before Him. Vanity comes into our life when our walk doesn't match the life of a blood-bought believer. It is SIN.

"The form in which the 3rd commandment is broken most completely, most awfully, most terribly, is by perpetually making use of the name of the Lord, while the life does not square with the profession made." **G. Campbell Morgan**

"Dear God, forgive me for taking your name in vain by using your name light-heartedly or by not living like the child of God that I am."

4th Commandment — Exodus 20:8-11 *"Remember the sabbath day, to keep it holy."*

"A person, especially one who professes to be a child of God, who believes he or she can engage in labor and self-interest seven days per week, week after week, and be just as well off spiritually as when they rested a day to give attention to spiritual nourishment, is not being realistic or honest." **Sam Davison**

We know that New Testament believers recognize Sunday as the Lord's Day. We sin, not in the remembering, but in the keeping it holy. Keeping it holy means to clean, dedicate, prepare, purify, and sanctify oneself wholly. There needs to be a preparation for the Lord's day. This day is not to be entered lukewarm and unprepared. In Exodus 19:10-11, the children of Israel took three days to clean up and prepare to meet with the Lord. Jesus gave His life for the church — *that* is how important it is to Him. Church life should be important to us. **Hebrews 10:25** *"Not forsaking the assembling of ourselves together, as the manner of some is; but exhorting one another: and so much the more, as ye see the day approaching."* It would behoove us to take it very seriously and to prepare for the Lord's day; anything less is called SIN.

"Dear God, forgive me for not keeping the Lord's day holy. Forgive me for approaching this day with a lukewarm attitude."

5th Commandment — Exodus 20:12 *"Honour thy father and thy mother:"*

> **Honour** = place in superiority, hold in high opinion, revere

This is the commandment with promise of a long life. All the days of their life, no matter the circumstances, we are to honor them. I do not know what it is like to be abused or mistreated by a parent. I do believe God will take care of any judgment that is to come on them. But I do not see an exception to this commandment. It is SIN when we are not honoring them.

Ephesians 6:2-3 *"Honour thy father and mother; (which is the first commandment with promise;) That it may be well with thee, and thou mayest live long on the earth."*

"Dear God, forgive me for not honoring my parents at all times."

6th Commandment — Exodus 20:13 *"Thou shalt not kill."*

Matthew 5:22 *"But I say unto you, That whosoever is angry with his brother without a cause shall be in danger of the judgment: and whosoever shall say to his brother, Raca, (worthless one) shall* *be in danger of the council: but whosoever shall say, Thou fool, shall be in danger of hell fire."*

I John 3:15 *"Whosoever hateth his brother is a murderer..."*

Hateth = to detest

Anger and hate toward someone is the attitude of murder. The words, "I hate them" should never come out of a Christian's mouth. When we get aggravated with someone and say in our heart, "She is an idiot," we are sinning. Having a critical spirit is a sin. It is SIN.

"Dear God, forgive me for committing murder in my heart and mind. Forgive me for having a critical spirit."

7th Commandment — Exodus 20:14 *"Thou shalt not commit adultery."*

Matthew 5:28 *"But I say unto you, That whosoever looketh on a woman to lust after her hath committed adultery with her already in his heart."*

Hebrews 13:4 *"Marriage is honourable in all, and the bed undefiled: but whoremongers and adulterers God will judge."*

We know God is serious concerning the sanctity of marriage. In today's society, adultery is excused and accepted. Most every family has been affected by adultery. It is prevalent in secular movies, books, and music. God says it should not even be in our thoughts. Adultery is still SIN.

"Dear God, forgive me for committing adultery in my heart and mind or ignoring it as though it were not an offense to you."

8th commandment — Exodus 20:15 *"Thou shalt not steal."*

We know it is not right to take something that does not belong to us. Most of us as children stole something; hopefully, we do not struggle with something so childish. But there is more "adult-like" stealing. There are verses that tell us that God has made us only stewards of what is rightly His. When we fail to tithe, we are stealing. When we do not have money to give because we have spent it all on ourselves, we are stealing. We are to be good stewards of all that God has entrusted to us. Our time, talents, and treasures are God's — not ours to do with what we want, not ours to steal from God's use. It is SIN when we waste any of these.

"Dear God, forgive me for stealing from you. Forgive me for self-indulgence. Forgive me for not being a good steward."

9th Commandment — Exodus 20:16 *"Thou shalt not bear false witness against thy neighbour."*

> **False witness =** lying, slander, gossip

Ephesians 4:29 *"Let no corrupt communication proceed out of your mouth, but that which is good to the use of edifying, that it may minister grace unto the hearers."*

This verse says "no" corrupt communication. We know "no" means none, zero, even to our best friend. This is a command, and we need to call gossip, slander, and lying what it is — and it is SIN.

"Dear God, forgive me for gossiping, for lying, and for saying anything that does not minister grace to the hearer."

10ᵗʰ Commandment — Exodus 20:17 *"Thou shalt not covet ..."*

> **Covet = desire, lust**

"We must understand that our coveting is not just a quiet, inward sin that robs us of contentment and joy. It is actually an assault of unbelief that is of great offense to God's name and character."
Melissa Kruger

Desiring something that is not ours, a house, husband (wife), housekeeper (servant), car (ass) is coveting. All of us can look at someone else's "things" and wish, and it can turn into covetousness in a hurry. Being discontent with *anything* in our life is a sin. It is SIN.

"Dear God, forgive me for coveting and not being satisfied with what you have given me. Forgive me for ever murmuring or complaining out of discontentment."

Matthew 22:37-38 *"Jesus said unto him, Thou shalt love the Lord thy God with all thy heart, and with all thy soul, and with all thy mind. This is the first and great commandment."*

We know that the first four commandments line up with loving God and that the following six line up with loving others. If we take a close look at these commandments, we will see that we break them regularly, and we need forgiveness. It is good to ask God to...**Psalm 139:22-24** *"Search me, O God, and know my heart: try me, and know my thoughts: And see if there be any wicked way in me, and lead me in the way everlasting."*

"Dear God, forgive me for breaking your commandments. Forgive me for my sin that you bore on the cross. Forgive me for sinning against you, for offending you. Forgive me for vanity and pride, for self-indulgence, for presuming upon your goodness, and for taking your blessings for granted. Forgive me for murmuring and complaining. Forgive me for having a critical spirit. I am not okay, and I need you to change me."

II Chronicles 7:14 *"If my people, which are called by my name, shall humble themselves, and pray, and seek my face, and turn from their wicked ways; then will I hear from heaven, and will forgive their sin, and will heal their land."*

"Remember the Ten Commandments. Believe the Ten Commandments. Love the Ten Commandments. Obey the Ten Commandments. Teach the Ten Commandments." **Sam Davison**

We had a Sunday school teacher workshop years ago, and we were taught the Ten Commandments by Gene Howard drawing them on a whiteboard, and I have known them ever since. Maybe his drawings will help you learn them and teach them.

THE TEN COMMANDMENTS

© Gene Howard — used with permission

Nothing Between

Charles A. Tindley 1905

Nothing between my soul and the Saviour
So that His blessed face may be seen;
Nothing preventing the least of His favor,
Keep the way clear!
Let nothing between.

Reflection:

Spend five minutes a day confessing your sin this week.

1 — False god; have no other gods

2 — Snake; no graven images

3 — Lips; do not use God's name in vain

4 — Church; remember the Sabbath and keep it holy

5 — Child; honor thy father and mother

6 — Gun; thou shalt not kill

7 — Broken home; thou shalt not commit adultery

8 — Robber's mask; thou shalt not steal

9 – "G" for gossip; thou shalt not bear false witness

10 – Person wanting the "O"; thou shalt not covet

Study to prepare for the next lesson:

Matthew 6:13a *"And lead us not into temptation, but deliver us from evil:"*

What is the definition of "deliver" according to Webster's 1828 dictionary?

What is the definition of "fast" according to Webster's 1828 dictionary?

Write out these verses: Psalm 70:5; Psalm 71:4; II Timothy 4:18.

When thou saidst,
Seek ye my face;
my heart said
unto thee, Thy face,
LORD, will I seek.
PSALM 27:8

6 *TEACH US TO PRAY FOR DELIVERANCE*

Matthew 6:13a *"And lead us not into temptation, but deliver us from evil…"*

"It is not as if God tempted any to sin; but, Lord, do not let Satan loose upon us; chain up that roaring lion, for he is subtle and spiteful; Lord, do not leave us to ourselves, for we are weak. Deliver us from ourselves, from our own evil hearts; deliver us from evil men." **Matthew Henry**

II Timothy 4:18 *"And the Lord shall deliver me from every evil work, and will preserve me unto his heavenly kingdom: to whom be glory for ever and ever. Amen."*

Warren Wiersbe says of this passage in II Timothy, "Paul's greatest fear was not of death; it was that he might deny his Lord or do something else that would disgrace God's name. He wanted to end his life well."

To deny or disgrace God should be our greatest fear also. How sad to come to the end of our lives and see that our lives were useless for God.

That is exactly what Satan wants to do —

render us useless for the work of God.

Psalm 70:5 *"But I am poor and needy: make haste unto me, O God: thou art my help and my deliverer; O LORD, make no tarrying."*

I need deliverance. We can pray that God would deliver us from the things that we just confessed, things that could render our lives useless for Him. I pray daily for my children that their lives will be delivered from Satan and his lies and from harm. I pray that their lives will be delivered from being rendered useless for God's service.

Bro. Sam Davison said that if much of our prayer time is not spent on praying for others, we do not have a very deep prayer life. We should pray for deliverance for the lost, for our family, for friends, for co-workers, for our pastor and his family, for our church staff, for our missionaries, for our country, etc. We can pray, "God, deliver….from harm and from Satan and his lies today. Deliver them from a life of uselessness."

There is no doubt that I have been delivered from myself and Satan and his lies because others cared enough to pray for me. We won't know, this side of heaven, the powerful impact that prayer has had on our lives.

However, the power of prayer is recorded for us in many accounts in the Bible. In the book of Esther, we see her praying for the deliverance of her people. **Esther 4:16** *"Go, gather together all the Jews that are present in Shushan, and fast ye for me, and neither eat nor drink three days, night or day: I also and my maidens will fast likewise; and so will I go in unto the king, which is not according to the law: and if I perish, I perish."* The burden on her heart was so heavy that she calls for a fast. God hears their prayers and delivers Esther and her people!

Throughout the Bible, fasting is mentioned with prayer; it is appropriate to fast and pray for deliverance. **Mark 9:29** and **Matthew 17:21** *"Howbeit this kind goeth not out but by prayer and fasting."*

Fasting doesn't guarantee that we will see any results of our prayers. King David fasted and prayed for his sick child — his son died. Fasting isn't for the purpose of God doing my will and me having my way. I have repeated this quote many times in this study, and I will again: "The biblical idea of prayer is that God's holiness, purpose, and wise order may be brought about**."** **Oswald Chambers**. We could reword it this way: "The biblical idea of *fasting* is that God's holiness, purpose and wise order may be brought about."

I wonder how serious we are about lost souls being saved? How serious are we about God's holiness and usefulness in our lives and in the lives of our children or fellow Christians? Many of our loved ones are in the bondage of sin. I wonder: if we were willing to fast for their deliverance, what could we see take place?

I cannot tell you how to fast or exactly how long you should fast. The Lord can teach us how to fast as He is teaching us to pray.

Following the examples in the Bible and the definitions are enough explanation to at least realize fasting along with prayer is appropriate and needful.

Webster's 1828 definition of fasting:

F'AST, *verb intransitive*

1. To abstain from food, beyond the usual time; to omit to take the usual meals, for a time; as, to *fast* a day or a week.

2. To abstain from food voluntarily, for the mortification of the body or appetites, or as a token of grief, sorrow, and affliction.

3. To abstain from food partially, or from particular kinds of food.

F'AST, *noun*

1. Abstinence from food; properly a total abstinence, but it is used also for an abstinence from particular kinds of food, for a certain time.

2. Voluntary abstinence from food, as a religious mortification or humiliation; either total or partial abstinence from customary food, with a view to mortify the appetites, or to express grief and affliction on account of some calamity, or to deprecate an expected evil.

Ezra 8:21 *"Then I proclaimed a fast there, at the river Ahava, that we might afflict ourselves before our God, to seek of him a right way for us, and for our little ones, and for all our substance."*

Daniel 9:3 *"And I set my face unto the Lord God, to seek by prayer and supplications, with fasting, and sackcloth, and ashes:"*

It says in Matthew "when ye fast," so we can see we are to fast. **Matthew 6:16-18** *"Moreover when ye fast, be not, as the hypocrites, of a sad countenance: for they disfigure their faces, that they may appear unto me to fast. Verily I say unto you, They have their reward. But thou, when thou fastest, anoint thine head, and wash thy face; That thou appear not unto me to fast, but unto the Father which is in secret: and thy Father, which seeth in secret, shall reward thee openly."*

Fasting is to depart from normal and take serious preparation because something is more important than eating. Does this mean enough to me to fast? So many are in need of deliverance, and we know the One who can deliver them, and us, from temptation and evil.

We need to be willing to fast at times. We need to be praying daily for deliverance from temptation and evil for others and ourselves –lest Satan renders us useless for the work of God!

What a Friend We Have in Jesus

Joseph M. Scrivner 1855

What a friend we have in Jesus,
All our sins and grief's to bear!
What a privilege to carry
Everything to God in prayer!
Oh, what peace we often forfeit,
Oh, what needless pain we bear,
All because we do not carry
Everything to God in prayer!

Have we trials and temptations?
Is there trouble anywhere?
We should never be discouraged—
Take it to the Lord in prayer.
Can we find a friend so faithful,
Who will all our sorrows share?
Jesus knows our every weakness;
Take it to the Lord in prayer.

Are we weak and heavy-laden,
Cumbered with a load of care?
Precious Savior, still our refuge —
Take it to the Lord in prayer.
Do thy friends despise, forsake thee?
Take it to the Lord in prayer!
In His arms He'll take and shield thee,
Thou wilt find a solace there.

Blessed Savior, Thou hast promised
Thou wilt all our burdens bear;
May we ever, Lord, be bringing
All to Thee in earnest prayer.
Soon in glory bright, unclouded,
There will be no need for prayer —
Rapture, praise, and endless worship
Will be our sweet portion there.

Reflection:

Spend five minutes a day praying for deliverance for others.

The greatest thing we could do for anyone is pray for them. Sometimes we can be overwhelmed by the needs of others. Here is a sample daily prayer list that might be a help:

Monday — Missionaries

Tuesday — Sunday school class

Wednesday — The church bulletin prayer list

Thursday — Salvation for the lost

Friday — Family, friends

Saturday — Our country

Sunday — Pastor and staff

Study to prepare for the next lesson:

Matthew 6:13b *"For thine is the kingdom, and the power, and the glory, for ever. Amen"*

Write out the following verses: Psalm 40:5; 139:14, 17-18; Isaiah 43:1; 49:15-16; Matthew 10:30.

Read I Chronicles 29:11-13.

According to a concordance, what does the word "praise" mean in I Chronicles 29:13?

I encourage you to read or listen to S.M. Lockridge's message, "That's My King" online. It will be a blessing! If you know Him, go ahead and praise Him!

When thou saidst,
Seek ye my face;
my heart said
unto thee, Thy face,
LORD, will I seek.

PSALM 27:8

7 *TEACH US TO PRAISE YOU*

Matthew 6:13b *"...For thine is the kingdom, and the power, and the glory, for ever. Amen."*

ALL THE PRAISE BELONGS TO HIM!

"It is just and equal; we praise God, and give Him glory, not because He needs it — He is praised by a world of angels — but because He deserves it; and it is our duty to give Him glory, in compliance with His design in revealing Himself to us."
Matthew Henry

I Chronicles 29:11-13 *"Thine, O LORD, is the greatness, and the power, and the glory, and the victory, and the majesty: for all that is in the heaven and in the earth is thine; thine is the kingdom, O LORD, and thou art exalted as head above all. Both riches and honour come of thee, and thou reignest over all; and in thine hand is power and might; and in thine hand it is to make great, and to* give strength unto all. Now therefore, our God, we thank thee, and praise thy glorious name."

Hebrews 13:15 *"By him therefore let us offer the sacrifice of praise to God continually, that is, the fruit of our lips giving thanks to his name."*

Psalm 97:1a *"The LORD reigneth; let the earth rejoice..."*

This part of the prayer is praise to God. This is the easy part of prayer. We do not need much of a lesson on how to praise God, or do we? Do you praise Him on purpose, regularly, daily?

We saw that we are to worship Him. **Matthew 6:9** *"...Our Father which art in heaven, Hallowed be thy name."* The posture of worship is low and humble.

Hallow = venerate = worship = prostrate oneself; get low; acknowledge the worth of another. Worship is humbling ourselves before Him, acknowledging who He is. But praising God looks quite different.

Praise = to shine; hence to make a show; to boast; to rave; to celebrate; to give thanks; to bless; to sing

---

So, go ahead and get excited about what He has done, and let the praise to Him burst forth from our lips. Go ahead and make a show, boast about Him, rave over Him, celebrate what He does for us!

Did you read or listen to S.M. Lockridge's message? Could you hear him saying, "That's my King, yeah."? I'm pretty sure he was making a show, boasting, raving, celebrating his King. Mmm, Mmm, Good!

Psalm 139:14, 17-18 *"I will praise thee; for I am fearfully and wonderfully made: marvelous are thy works; and that my soul knoweth right well. How precious also are thy thoughts unto me, O God! how great is the sum of them! If I should count them, they are more in number than the sand: when I awake, I am still with thee."*

Isaiah 43:1 *"But now thus saith the LORD that created thee, O Jacob, and he that formed thee, O Israel, Fear not: for I have redeemed thee, I have called thee by thy name; thou art mine."*

Isaiah 49:15-16a *"Can a woman forget her sucking child, that she should not have compassion on the son of her womb? yea, they may forget, yet will I not forget thee. Behold, I have graven thee upon the palms of my hands..."*

Matthew 10:30 *"But the very hairs of your head are all numbered."*

He knows our name. He is a personal God. We should never "get over" the fact that the God of the universe wants a personal relationship with us. He loves us! He is worthy of our praise!

Do you remember the day you were saved? God called *your* name, He singled *you* out, He sought *you*!

We sing the chorus, "Thank you, Lord, for saving my soul. Thank you, Lord, for making me whole. Thank you, Lord, for giving to me thy great salvation so rich and free." **Seth Sykes**

Do you remember the day He saved *your* soul? Will you take a minute and reflect on when you were saved? Can you get excited about what God has done? Go ahead and make a show, boast about Him, rave over Him; celebrate what He has done for you!

"Thank you, Lord, for making me **whole**." We were undone, lost in sin, without hope, and He made us whole. We were like Lazarus, bound in grave clothes. Can you get excited that He has made you whole? Go ahead and make a show, boast about Him, rave over Him; celebrate what He has done for you!

"Thank you, Lord, for **giving** to me..." Salvation was a gift! Can you get excited about this priceless, eternal, forever, gift? Go ahead and make a show, boast about Him, rave over Him; celebrate what He has done for you!

"Thy **great** salvation, so **rich,** and free." This great and rich salvation is a personal relationship with Him. He walks with us and talks with us! We do not have to wait 'till we get to Heaven! Can you get excited about what He has done? Go ahead and make a show, boast about Him, rave over Him; celebrate what He does for you!

How rich are you? The book of Ephesians has been called the "Be Rich" book by Warren Wiersbe. **Ephesians 1:3, 6-7** *"Blessed be the God and Father of our Lord Jesus Christ, who hath blessed us with all spiritual blessings in heavenly places in Christ: To the praise of the glory of his grace, wherein he hath made us accepted in the beloved. In whom we have redemption through his blood, the forgiveness of sins, according to the riches of his grace;"*

"True riches come from God. It is a source of great encouragement to know that Father, Son, and Holy Spirit are all working on my behalf to make me rich. God not only gives us "richly all things to enjoy" (I Tim. 6:17), but He gives us eternal riches, without which all other wealth is valueless."
Warren Wiersbe

Psalm 40:5 *"Many, O LORD my God, are thy wonderful works which thou hast done, and thy thoughts which are to us-ward: they cannot be reckoned up in order unto thee: if I would declare and speak of them, they are more than can be numbered."*

A few years ago, Bro. Dave Hardy preached a message on thankfulness, and he challenged us with this quote, "If today you woke up with what you thanked God for yesterday, what would you still have?"

Psalm 67:3 *"Let the people praise thee, O God; let all the people praise thee."* (praise = give thanks)

Psalm 35:18 *"I will give thee thanks in the great congregation: I will praise thee among much people."* (praise= to shine; hence to make a show)

With the Psalmist, let us say, "I *WILL* PRAISE YOU, LORD! I will make a show, boast about YOU, rave over YOU, celebrate what YOU have done and do for me!"

Psalm 103:1 *"Bless the LORD, O my soul: and all that is within me, bless his holy name."*

The circumstances of life should not dictate whether or not we praise God. When we stop and praise Him for all He has done and is doing and will do — we could never praise Him enough!

The Love of God

Hope Publishing 1923

The love of God is greater far than tongue or pen can ever tell.

It goes beyond the highest star and reaches to the lowest hell.

The guilty pair, bowed down with care, God gave His Son to win;

His erring child He reconciled and pardoned from his sin.

O love of God, how rich and pure!

How measureless and strong!

It shall forevermore endure the saints' and angels' song.

When hoary time shall pass away, and earthly thrones and kingdoms fall;

When men who here refuse to pray, on rocks and hills and mountains call;

God's love, so sure, shall still endure, all measureless and strong;

Redeeming grace to Adams's race-the saints' and angels' song.

Could we with ink the ocean fill, and were the skies of parchment made;

Were every stalk on earth a quill, and every man a scribe by trade;

To write the love of God above would drain the ocean dry;

Nor could the scroll contain the whole, though stretched from sky to sky.

73

Refection:

Spend five minutes a day praising and thanking God this week.

Study to prepare for the next lesson:

Matthew 6:13c *"...Amen."*

According to a concordance, what does the word "Amen" mean in Matthew 6:13?

Write out these verses: II Chronicles 7:14; Jeremiah 33:3; and James 5:16.

When thou saidst,
Seek ye my face;
my heart said
unto thee, Thy face,
LORD, will I seek.

PSALM 27:8

8 *THE AMEN*

Matthew 6:13c *". . . Amen."*

This last chapter is a final challenge to be a Christian who prays. Jesus ends the prayer with, "Amen." The word "Amen" means we are agreeing with the Word. It is to say, "So be it, surely, this is truth." I do pray that, as you come to the end of this study, you can agree with the Word that these timeless biblical principles are truth. Not just agree that they are truth but be a doer of what we have been challenged with out of God's Word. PRAY!

We started this study with **Psalm 27:8** *"...When thou saidst, Seek ye my face; my heart said unto thee, Thy face, LORD, will I seek."*

"David is telling of the satisfaction and benefit he experienced from seeking God's face, from communing with God in prayer." **Matthew Henry**

"The biblical idea of prayer is that God's holiness, purpose, and

wise order may be brought about." Oswald Chambers

That is what this Bible study has been about — a prayer life that will satisfy and benefit our lives so that God's holiness, purpose, and wise order may be brought about in our lives.

"There is no place where the devil so resists us as when we pray!" **R.A. Torrey**

I listened to a message on prayer by David Gibbs in which he said, "Prayer is the most powerful thing in the universe." He asked, "How many of you want your prayer life to have the power of God?" He also said, "There are things we all want for our family, church, country, self, but we do not pray. We have not because we ask not." He gives four keys to our prayer life having the power of God.

James 5:16b "... *The effectual fervent prayer of a righteous man availeth much."*

> *You have to pray. (We have to ask!)
> *Be fervent, pour yourself into it. (Pray for an hour — fast?)
> *Get clean, be righteous. (If we have a fervent prayer life, we will get clean.)
> *Persist — praying last week is not enough.

"Back again to the wide-eyed wonder of a child at God's answers to our prayers." **Oswald Chambers**

"Effective prayer is the provision for every need and the solution for every problem." **Warren Wiersbe**

The woman whose book I read that challenged me to spend an hour with God every day said she made a daily appointment with God. She got a cup of coffee and her Bible and a notebook. She read her Bible, expecting to hear from God. She wrote out the verses that spoke to her, and then she wrote out her prayer. She saw God do great and mighty things. **Jeremiah 33:3** "Call unto me, and I will answer thee, and shew thee great and mighty things, which thou knowest not."

I do not have the patience to write out my prayers. I have challenged myself to be better at journaling this time with God and to keep track of answered prayer.

After keeping my appointments with God, daily, I found that I wanted more. I have to say it is the most satisfying and beneficial time of my life. There is absolutely nothing else I could do with that hour that would benefit those on my prayer list or me more!

Pray? Yes, because we are a very needy people. What is our greatest need? That God's holiness, purpose, and wise order may be brought about in our life!

"A thing is worth just what it cost. Prayer is not what it costs us but what it cost God to enable us to pray. Beware of placing the emphasis on what prayer cost us. It cost God everything to make it possible for us to pray." **Oswald Chambers**

I believe it was from the Personal Spiritual Development class at Heartland Baptist Bible College where I first heard the challenge of spending an hour in prayer using Matthew 6.

One hour of prayer:

10 minutes – Worship – Matthew 6:9

10 minutes – Surrender – Matthew 6:10

10 minutes – Dependence – Matthew 6:11

10 minutes – Repentance – Matthew 6:12

10 minutes – Deliverance – Matthew 6:13a

10 minutes – Praise & Thanksgiving – Matthew 6:13b

I challenge you to have an hour of prayer using this format, soon, while this study is still fresh in your mind. It will be the best hour you have ever spent!

I don't know about you, but I really don't want to miss out on God's wonderful works because I didn't choose to seek His face in a meaningful prayer time!

"All our failures are prayer failures." **John R. Rice**

"A thing is worth just what it cost. Prayer is not what it costs us, but what it cost God to enable us to pray." **Oswald Chambers**

"Prayer can do anything that God can do, and, as God can do anything, prayer is omnipotent." **R. A. Torrey**

"If you are not praying, you might as well be an atheist because you are living like you don't need God." **Unknown**

"The biblical idea of prayer is that God's holiness, purpose, and wise order may be brought about." Oswald Chambers

AMEN!

Sweet Hour of Prayer

W.W. Walford 1845

Sweet hour of prayer! Sweet hour of prayer!
That calls me from a world of care,
And bids me at my Father's throne
Make all my wants and wishes known.
In seasons of distress and grief,
My soul has often found relief
And oft escaped the tempter's snare
By thy return, sweet hour of prayer!

Sweet hour of prayer! Sweet hour of prayer!
The joys I feel, the bliss I share,
Of those whose anxious spirits burn
With strong desires for thy return!
With such I hasten to the place
Where God my Savior shows His face,
And gladly take my station there,
And wait for thee, sweet hour of prayer!

Sweet hour of prayer! Sweet hour of prayer!
Thy wings shall my petition bear
To Him whose truth and faithfulness
Engage the waiting soul to bless.
And since He bids me seek His face,
Believe His Word and trust His grace,
I'll cast on Him my every care,
And wait for thee, sweet hour of prayer!

Sweet hour of prayer! Sweet hour of prayer!
May I thy consolation share,
Till, from Mount Pisgah's lofty height,
I view my home and take my flight:
This robe of flesh I'll drop and rise
To seize the everlasting prize;
And shout, while passing through the air,
"Farewell, farewell, sweet hour of prayer!"

God's simple plan of salvation:

Romans 3:23 *"For all have sinned, and come short of the glory of God;"*

Romans 6:23 *"For the wages of sin is death; but the gift of God is eternal life through Jesus Christ our Lord."*

Romans 5:8 *"But God commendeth his love toward us, in that, while we were yet sinners, Christ died for us."*

Romans 10:9, 10, 13 *"That if thou shalt confess with thy mouth the Lord Jesus, and shalt believe in thine heart that God hath raised him from the dead thou shalt be saved. For with the heart man believeth unto righteousness; and with the mouth confession is made unto salvation. For whosoever shall call upon the name of the Lord shall be saved."*

If you are not yet a child of God, and you cannot call Him "Father" all you need to do is admit your sin and trust in Jesus. Simply pray to God and ask Him to forgive you and to save you.

When thou saidst,
Seek ye my face;
my heart said
unto thee, Thy face,
LORD, will I seek.

PSALM 27:8

About the Author

Anita was raised in an Independent Baptist preacher's home and is one of eleven children. She was saved at the age of eight. She has served as a Sunday school teacher for 38 years and has volunteered in the Oklahoma Jail and Prison Ministry for 18 years. Anita was married to her high school sweetheart for 12 years before he was killed in an accident at work. God gave them three children, whom the Lord helped Anita raise as a single mom. They are all faithful and serve the Lord. Her children and eight grandchildren are the joy of her life.

Made in the USA
Columbia, SC
10 January 2020